A Mother's Prayers

By Jayanti Reid Manigat

D1383152

Foreword by Sister Gwen Shaw

PRESS

www.xulonpress.com

Endorsements

❧❧

"Jayanti examines the body of a child and releases blessings through Scripture in *A Mother's Prayers*. You can clearly hear God's heart of love for His children as she details the power of the Holy Spirit through Scripture. This is an interesting journey of powerful blessings being imparted as the Word is spoken over the children, developing the Holy Spirit within them. As these Scriptures are prayed and imparted, the children will grow into the character and nature of Christ because it has become a part of them. This is a must-read for all mothers to use as a guideline to nurture their children."

—Bonnie Jones, Bob Jones Ministries

"Jayanti's prayers of blessing and petition beautifully capture the essence of a mother's heart, expressed with intercession. She raises an inspiring standard for all mothers of unyielding determination and unconditional love mixed with complete dependence on and trust in our almighty Father."

—Julie Joyner, Morningstar Ministries

Contents

Dedication

I dedicate this book to all mothers. As you bathe and cleanse the body parts of your child, speak to each part of your child's body. Pronounce a blessing over your child to each part of his body. This book will guide you to speak words of affirmation to your child. As mothers, our primary obligation is to encourage and nourish a child as he grows in the ways of God, both spiritually and physically.

Forewords

Jayanti expresses the true sentiments of a mother's heart in this beautiful prayer book. It reminds me of my own feelings when I held my firstborn in my arms. Oh, the wonder of it all! I could hardly grasp the fact that this beautiful creation of God's had come out of my body, that God and I had worked together to create this "world wonder," and that it had taken only nine months to put such a living miracle together!

Every mother should read it. But I especially recommend it to expectant mothers and to those who find themselves with an unwanted pregnancy. It would be impossible to abort such a gift from God.

This book should be given out to women going into abortion clinics, hospitals, doctors' offices, schools, and youth groups.

Thank you, Jayanti, for reminding us of the greatest miracle of life—the birthing of our children.

Gwen R. Shaw, Th.D., D.D.
Founder and president of End-Time Handmaidens

Jayanti has written a precious manuscript that is loaded with gems of Holy Spirit-inspired prayers that you can use as a guide to pray for your own children. As a loving and caring mother, Jayanti reveals a prophetic tenderness that is expressed through the eyes of a watchful mother, much like a mother eagle that watches over her young. This book is needed in the perilous days in which our children are being raised. The prayers that Jayanti uses and shares with you will bring protection, anointing, strength, health, and mental brilliance to your children. Be prepared for God's blessings to come upon your children in a new and powerful way as you apply the principles found in this book.

Reverend Steven Brooks
Moravian Falls, North Carolina

Preface

❦

All parents who desire their children to grow into well-balanced maturity should read this book.

Harsh or critical words can affect a child throughout his or her life in a negative way. However, words of blessing and encouragement will affect a child in a positive, creative way. As you read, become aware that the outcome of your child's life is fashioned during the early, formative years.

As you absorb the pages that follow, you will be both challenged and blessed with the wisdom of a mother's love for her child.

Wade E. Taylor,
Wade Taylor Ministries

Introduction

The wise woman builds her house.

Proverbs 14:1 NIV

The moment I saw you, my precious child, I gave thanks to God our Father for giving me the privilege and honor of being your mother. I have treasured each day of my life spent with you.

As I held you in my arms, I was mesmerized by God's created beauty and workmanship, in creating you. I carefully examined every detail about you. I caressed your soft skin, perfect, without blemish. I looked very closely at you in amazement of your beauty.

I ran my fingers back and forth through your silky black hair, shiny and full of nourishment. You had a full head of hair. It was very soft. Your hair was beautiful, like shining diamonds.

As I looked into your beautiful brown eyes, it was as though I was seeing the purity in you. I felt that I was seeing God through your eyes. They were very expressive. I received so much comfort from looking at your eyes; I felt as though they were telling me, "Mommy, it will be okay." Your eyes were an expression of love, peace, joy, and tranquility. I spent many hours looking at you through your eyes, wondering what you were thinking. If you could only speak, tell me if there was a message from God, tell me what God looks like . . . I know that you have seen Him and been with Him; if I could just read your mind . . .

Your nose, small and beautiful, reminded me of your father's. As you took a breath, I realized the Lord God is within you and the spirit of God is in your nostrils, as God made man from the dust of the ground and breathed into his nostrils the breath of life. I praise *Elohim*—God the Creator—for you.

Your ears were so attentive. They were telling me that you were still hearing the sounds of heaven—the music coming from the heavenly realm sung by the chorus of angels. All the bells in heaven were ringing, and all the angels in heaven were rejoicing, for you were born. It marked a special day on the calendar, as you are now on the Earth. As I ran my index finger over your ears, I spoke to you the words "Welcome to Earth."

Your lips are perfectly shaped. They are your father's lips, kissable and soft. I must have kissed you a hundred times before I gently placed you back in your bed. Your lips tasted as sweet as honeycomb. As I looked at your lips, it was as though you said to me, "Mama, one day I will speak the oracles of God." I realized that your lips are anointed with grace. Your lips are like lilies dripping with myrrh. Your mouth is sweetness itself, for your lips proclaim the name of the Lord Jesus.

Your hands were very soft and delicate. They were fragile and small. I placed your hands on my lips, and I realized God's handiwork has reached a marvelous depth and breadth. You extended your hands toward me, and that showed me a complete expression of God's love. I wept as I realized the fingerprints of the Almighty God are in you, as He made you.

Your feet were tender and tiny. I gazed upon your toes; they were fairer than a diadem. I kissed your feet tenderly; they were soft like cotton clouds of heaven. I knew these feet had walked in heavenly places with Jesus along the streets of gold. I thanked the Father God that these feet were now on Earth and you would walk together with me.

The Helmet of Salvation

"Thou . . . Art a Shield"

As You created man, holy Father, you gave him the head to be the top portion of his body. Lord Jesus, you are the head, the covering for every man, the shield to our head. Father, I thank You for this child. "Thou, O LORD, art a shield for [him; his] glory, and the lifter up of [his] head" (Psalm 3:3).

We bless Your name, Lord Jesus. My child bows down his head and worships You (Genesis 24:26). "Thine, O LORD, is the greatness, and the power, and the glory, and the victory, and the majesty: for all that is in the heaven and in the earth is thine; thine is the kingdom, O LORD, and thou art exalted as head above all" (1 Chronicles 29:11).

I thank You, Lord, that You welcome my child with rich blessings and placed a crown of pure gold on his head (Psalm 21:3). Thank You, Lord, that You anoint my child's head with oil (Psalm 23:5). It is like the precious ointment upon his head (Psalm 133:2). I thank You, Lord, that blessings are upon the head of my child (Proverbs 10:6). You have made him the head and not the tail. He is above and not beneath (Deuteronomy 28:13).

The Mind of Christ

Amazing are your wonders, oh Lord. Who can fathom Your creation? You created the mind of a person uniquely. A mind of a person can do great things that cause people to marvel at the gift of creativity You gave him. With the mind, a person can offer the world new discoveries. The wealth and richness of a person are all in the mind, yielded to You, Lord Jesus. I thank God, through Jesus Christ our Lord! "So then with the mind [my child serves] the law of God" (Romans 7:25).

Thank You, Lord Jesus, for my child has known the mind of the Lord, so You, Lord, may instruct him, for he has the mind of Christ (1 Corinthians 2:16). Thank You, Lord Jesus, that my child's delight is in the law of the Lord, and on Your law, He meditates day and night (Psalm 1:2). Thank You, Lord Jesus, that my child is like a tree planted by streams of water that yields its fruit in season and whose leaf does not wither. Whatever he does prospers (Psalm 1:3).

I thank You, Lord Jesus, that You know the thoughts of my child (Psalm 94:11). You know, Lord, when my child sits and when he rises; you perceive the thoughts from afar (Psalm 139:2). How great are your works, O Lord; how profound your thoughts (Psalm 92:5). Isaiah 55:8-9 declares: "For my thoughts are not your thoughts, neither are your ways my ways. . . . As the heavens are higher than the earth, so are my ways higher than your ways, and my thoughts than your thoughts." I bless my child that he will set his mind on things above, not on earthly things (Colossians 3:2).

Father, I ask that You help my child, that he "might walk worthy of the Lord unto all pleasing, being fruitful in every good work, and increasing in the knowledge of God" (Colossians 1:10).

Every Hair Is Numbered

As I shampoo my child's hair, I thank You, Lord Jesus, for every hair on my child's head, which is numbered (Matthew 10:30). Your Word says, "Are not two sparrows sold for a penny? Yet not one of them will fall to the ground apart from the will of your Father. And even the very hairs of your head are all numbered. So don't be afraid; you are worth more than many sparrows" (Matthew 10:29-31 NIV).

Lord Jesus, as I carefully brush each strand of my child's hair, I am reminded of Your goodness toward my child. Each strand of his hair is precious to You. If my child lost one hair strand, You know about it, Lord. You made him beautiful. No one in this world has the same hair as he does. He is uniquely and wonderfully made.

I thank You, Lord Jesus, that You created my child's inmost being; You knit my child together in my womb. I praise You, Lord Jesus, because my child is fearfully and wonderfully made; wonderful are Your works, Lord Jesus, his inner self knows full well (Psalm 139:13-15). Lord Jesus, accept this humble act of worship as I bow down and kiss Your feet.

Children are a blessing from You. Holy Father, I am grateful to You for my children. As Mary took "a pound of ointment of spikenard, very costly, and anointed" Your feet, Lord Jesus, "and wiped [Your] feet with her hair: and the house was filled with the odour of the ointment," so will my child honor You, Lord Jesus (John 12:3). As my child watches me worship You, may this serve as an example to him, to bow down and kiss Your feet, anoint Your feet with oil, and wipe Your feet with our hair. May I be a good example to him, teaching him to worship You in reverence and truth.

2

Hearing of God's Glory

❧

As I clean my child's ear, I thank You, Lord Jesus, that my child will listen carefully to Your voice and will do what is right in Your eyes. He will pay attention to Your commands and keep all Your decrees (Exodus 15:26). I thank You, Lord Jesus, that my child will hear "how great you are, O Sovereign Lord!" He will hear "there is no one like you, and there is no God but you" (2 Samuel 7:22 NIV). My child's ear will receive a whisper of secrets You bring to him (Job 4:12).

Lord Jesus, I ask that You grant my child the discernment to know Your voice, the sweet whisper of Your voice. Allow him to recognize that it is You, his holy Father, speaking to him, directing him. Lord Jesus, You call Your own sheep by their name, and You lead them out. You say, "This is the way; walk in it" (Isaiah 30:21 NIV). You are the Good Shepherd, and the sheep know Your voice, and he will follow. I thank You, Lord Jesus, that my child will listen to Your voice. He will not follow a stranger's voice, but will run away from a stranger because he does not recognize the stranger's voice (John 10:3-5). Just as Samuel, at a very early age, heard Your voice and recognized that it was You, Lord, speaking to him, so will my child say, "[Lord,] speak, for your servant is listening" (1 Samuel 3:10). He will hear and understand Your word (Job 13:1).

Help my child, Lord Jesus, to recognize by the power of the Holy Spirit living in him to know and to have unction of what is from You and what is not from You. Allow him to rebuke and to cast away what he may hear that is not from You. As my child hears of the things that go on in this world and hears the voices of the people around him, protect his ears, Lord Jesus, from the voice of the enemy (Matthew 6:13). And I ask for Your promise to deliver him from temptation (2 Peter 2:9).

Your ears, Lord, are attentive to hear his cry (Psalm 18:6). As he calls upon You, Lord, You will hear his voice, and his cry will come upon Your ears (2 Samuel 22:7). Grant my child, Lord, Your mercy; accept his prayers (Psalm 6:9). Give his ears clarity and a good understanding.

May his ears remember the teaching I give him (Proverbs 4:20). I bless my child that he will keep Your decrees and commands, so it may go well with my child and he may prosper in all he does and wherever he goes (Deuteronomy 4:40; 1 Kings 2:3).

3

The Breath of Life

As I clean my child's nose, I thank You, Lord Jesus, that, as Genesis 2:7 says, "the LORD God formed the man from the dust of the ground and breathed into his nostrils the breath of life, and the man became a living being." Lord Jesus, You created my child, and I will forever be grateful to You. I will thank You, Lord Jesus, for as long as my child has life within him, the breath of God in his nostrils (Job 27:3). I praise You, Lord Jesus, that the Spirit of God has made my child; the breath of the Almighty gives him life (Job 33:4). It is the Spirit in a man, the breath of the Almighty that gives him understanding (Job 32:8). I praise You, Lord Jesus, for the breath of life You gave my child. Let everything that has breath and every breath of life praise the Lord! (Psalm 150:6).

I give You thanks, Lord Jesus, for each day I spend with my child. Life is more beautiful and more meaningful to me as I spend each day with my child. "This is the day the Lord has made; [I will] rejoice and be glad in it" (Psalm 118:24 NIV).

I thank You, Lord Jesus, that You have protected my child against any attacks of the enemy. My child is breathing well. You sustain life with the air that we breathe. I thank You, holy Father, that my child will grow well, and be full in stature, mighty, and strong, for he breathes life each day yielded and consecrated unto You, Lord Jesus.

4

A Beautiful Sight

As I gaze upon my child's eyes, I thank You, Lord Jesus, for these beautiful eyes You have made. I am mesmerized by the beauty I see. It is as though my child is saying to me, "Mama, my eyes have seen Jesus." As I look through my child's eyes, I feel God's love and tenderness. My child's eyes are a window through which I feel God's affection. Through the eyes of a child, I receive great joy in knowing that my God loves me.

I thank You, Lord Jesus, that I have found favor in You and my child has found grace in Your eyes (Genesis 6:8). Lord Jesus, help me as I train up my child to walk in Your ways, so that "when he is old, he will not depart from it" (Proverbs 22:6). Enable me to be a good example to him and set a good moral foundation for him to follow. Thank You, Lord Jesus, that my child will abide by Deuteronomy 11:18:

"Therefore you shall lay up these words of mine in your [mind and] heart and in your [entire being], and bind them as a sign on your hand and they shall be as frontlets between your eyes" (NKJV). I bless my child, Lord Jesus, that he will be obedient to Your words in Deuteronomy 13:18: "When thou shalt hearken to the voice of the LORD thy God, to keep all his commandments which I command thee this day, to do that which is right in the eyes of the LORD thy God."

Your Word tells us, "The eye is the lamp of the body. If your eyes are good, your whole body will be full of light" (Matthew 6:22 NIV). Protect the eyes of my child, Lord Jesus, from evil; protect his eyes from seeing anything that is not pleasing to You. Keep his eyes pure. Help him to stay focused on You. Your Word tells us in Isaiah 26:3, "You will keep him in perfect peace, whose mind is stayed on You, because he trusts in you" (NKJV). Help my child, Lord Jesus, to keep his eyes focused on You. "Let your eyes look directly ahead and let your gaze be fixed straight in front of you" (Proverbs 4:25). May the sweet Holy Spirit help my child not to be distracted and not to spend his time and energy on things that are not helping him fulfill his destiny, "looking unto [You, Lord] Jesus the author and finisher of our faith" (Hebrews 12:2).

As he looks unto You, Lord Jesus, the glory of Your image will be imprinted on him. May he find his true identity in You, Lord. The way You see him, Lord Jesus, through the eyes of his Maker, is not the way man sees him, for man looks at the outward appearance, but God looks at the heart (1 Samuel 16:7). Give him the confidence to see himself as valuable; his self-worth is pleasing in the eyes of his heavenly Father, for he is the image and the glory of God (1 Corinthians 11:7).

Lord Jesus, give my child the peace and security of knowing that he is accepted, not rejected, by You. Free him from the self-focus and the self-conscious-ness that can imprison his soul. Help him to see who You really are so he'll know who he really is. May his true self-image be the image of Christ stamped upon his soul. Your Word tells us in 2 Corinthians 3:18, "We all, with unveiled face, beholding as in a mirror the glory of the Lord, are being transformed into the same image from glory to glory, just as by the Spirit of the Lord" (NKJV).

I bless my child, and I proclaim over him, "Arise, shine; for your light has come! And the glory of the LORD is risen upon you" (Isaiah 60:1, NKJV). Thank You, Lord Jesus, that my child will see visions and will dream dreams as You pour out Your Spirit upon his flesh (Acts 2:17).

I ask, Lord Jesus, that as You spoke unto Moses face to face, as a man speaks unto his friend (Exodus 33:11), my child's eyes will see You clearly, and his eyes will not go dim (Deuteronomy 34:7). Blessed are the eyes of my child, for they are sealed for You, holy Father.

5

Speak the Truth in Love

As I brush my child's teeth, I thank You, Lord Jesus, that the lips of my child are like a scarlet ribbon; his mouth is lovely (Song of Solomon 4:3). His lips are like lilies dripping with myrrh (Song of Solomon 5:13). His mouth is like the best wine (Song of Solomon 7:9). I thank You, Lord Jesus, that my child has received favor from You and Your loving-kindness shines upon my child (Genesis 19:19). As it says in Your Word, "You are fairer than the sons of men; Grace is poured upon Your lips; Therefore God has blessed You forever" (Psalm 45:2 NKJV). "Because Your lovingkindness is better than life, My lips shall praise You" (Psalm 63:3 NKJV). The mouth of my child "shall praise You with joyful lips" (Psalm 63:5 NKJV). His lips shall greatly rejoice when he sings unto You, Lord, for his soul, You have redeemed (Psalm 71:23). Thank You, Lord

Jesus, that You have given my child a special voice to speak Your oracles and to declare Your Word in the gift of singing. You have given my child a great talent; the ability to make music has come from You. I rejoice in great delight when I hear my child sing. It fills our home with a merry sound. It brings great honor and unspeakable joy in my spirit when I hear my child shout out the word "hallelujah." It makes me a very proud mother to know that my child's lips bring honor to Your name.

As my child grows up and gets around other children to play with and other adults in the community, I ask, Lord Jesus, that You protect my child from the bad language or ungodly speech that he hears from the people around him. The good things of life seem to overlook those who have nothing good coming out of their mouths. Help him, Lord, to know that this is not pleasing to You and not to enter into the trap of evil language coming from his lips. "Let all bitterness, and wrath, and anger, and clamour, and evil speaking, be put away from you, with all malice" (Ephesians 4:31). Set a guard, Lord Jesus, over the mouth of my child; keep watch over the door of his lips (Psalm 141:3). Put away perversities from his mouth, Lord; keep corrupt talk far from his lips (Proverbs 4:24).

Help my child to obey joyfully when he is asked to do something. "Do all things without complaining and disputing, that you may become blameless and harmless, children of God without fault in the midst of a crooked and perverse generation, among whom you shine as lights in the world" (Philippians 2:14-15 NKJV).

May his mouth speak what is true, and his lips detest wickedness (Proverbs 8:7). Right and just lips are the delight of a king, and he loves "him who speaks what is right" (Proverbs 16:13 NKJV). "A wise man's heart guides his mouth, and his lips promote instruction" (Proverbs 16:23 NIV). I thank You, Lord Jesus, that "the law from your mouth is more precious to [my child] than thousands of pieces of silver and gold" (Psalm 119:72 NIV). I thank You, Lord Jesus, that my child will not let the Book of the Law depart from his mouth; he will "meditate on it day and night, so that [he] may be careful to do everything written in it. Then [he] will be prosperous and successful" (Joshua 1:8 NIV). I bless the lips of my child, and I know that the Word of Christ dwell in him richly in all wisdom (Colossians 3:16).

6

Blessed Are the Hands
of My Child

As I wash my child's hands, I thank You, Lord Jesus, for these blessed hands. You made these fingers; thank You, holy Father, for these beautiful fingers. "I consider your heavens, the work of your fingers, the moon and the stars, which you have set in place" (Psalm 8:3 NIV). "I sing for joy at the works of your hands" (Psalm 92:4 NIV). Forever I love you, Lord Jesus. I thank You, Lord Jesus, that "Your hands made [my child] and formed [him; you gave him] understanding to learn your commands" (Psalm 119:73). I thank You, Lord Jesus, that "you made him ruler over the works of your hands; you put everything under his feet" (Psalm 8:6 NIV). You gave my child power and authority over unclean spirits, to drive them out, and to cure all kinds of disease and all kinds of weakness and infirmity (Matthew 10:1).

"Heal the sick, cleanse the lepers, raise the dead, cast out devils: freely ye have received, freely give" (Matthew 10:8).

Thank You, Lord Jesus, that You gave us hands, so that we may extend Your love and grace toward others. It is a lovely sight in Your eyes when we use our hands to bless another person, and when we use our hands to give a hug to a hurting friend, to help comfort. Blessed are the hands of my child, for he will use them to love. Help him, Lord Jesus, not to use his hands to harm or to strike another child. May others feel Your love through my child's hands, as he extends them to help another person.

I thank You, Lord Jesus, that You will deal with my child according to his righteousness; according to the cleanness of his hands You will reward him (Psalm 18:20). Psalm 24:3-5 says, "Who shall ascend into the hill of the LORD? Or who shall stand in his holy place? He that hath clean hands, and a pure heart; who hath not lifted up his soul unto vanity, nor sworn deceitfully. He shall receive the blessing from the LORD, and righteousness from the God of his salvation." He will wash his hands "in innocence, and go about your altar, O LORD" (Psalm 26:6 NIV). He will bless you, Lord Jesus, while he lives; he will lift up his hands in Your name (Psalm 63:4).

7

On the Right Path

❦❦

As I place the socks and shoes on my child's feet, I thank You, Lord Jesus, for these beautiful feet You have made. These tiny feet are precious like diamonds; You have made them like rubies and gems. I have watched these feet grow in size and width. I look back at the shoes he has worn—I have saved them in the attic—from his first shoes, going forward to the different shoe sizes he has worn through the months and years. It amazes me. Only You, Lord Jesus, can help him grow in perfect size and width. My child has a good composure and will continue to grow full in stature.

I thank You, Lord Jesus, that the sweet Holy Spirit will guide my child to go to places where You destined for him to be. As You did for Paul and his companions, so You will guide the feet of my child as well (Acts 16:7-9). Your Word declares in Job 13:27,

"You fasten my feet in shackles; you keep close watch on all my paths by putting marks on the soles of my feet" (NIV). Thank You, Lord Jesus, that You keep a close watch over my child. Protect my child, Lord Jesus, from going to places that are not safe for him. Protect him from evil. Do not allow my child to get hurt or to be in any type of danger. I declare Your words in Psalm 18:36: "Thou hast enlarged my steps under me, that my feet did not slip." I thank You, Lord Jesus, that the sweet Holy Spirit will keep my child on the highway of holiness so that he will walk worthy of the calling with which he is called, "with all lowliness and gentleness, with longsuf-fering, bearing with one another in love" (Ephesians 4:1-2 NKJV). I ask You, Lord Jesus, that You will refrain my child's feet "from every evil way, that [he] may keep Your word (Psalm 119:101 NKJV). "Your word is a lamp to [his] feet and a light to [his] path (Psalm 119:105 NKJV). I ask You, Lord Jesus, to "ponder the path of [my child's] feet, and let all [his] ways be established. Turn not to the right hand nor to the left: remove [his] foot from evil" (Proverbs 4:26-27). My child's steps are ordered by You, Lord, and he delighted in Your ways (Psalm 37:23).

I am proud of my child, for it says in Isaiah 52:7, "How beautiful on the mountains are the feet of those who bring good news, who proclaim peace, who bring good tidings, who proclaim salvation, who say to Zion, 'Your God reigns!'" (NIV). I ask, Lord Jesus, that You will speak to my child as it says in Ezekiel 2:1-2: "He said to me, 'Son of man, stand up on your feet and I will speak to you.' As he spoke, the Spirit came into me and raised me to my feet, and I heard him speaking to me" (NIV).

Thank You, Lord Jesus, that You will enable my child to be strong, as it says in Habakkuk 3:19: "The Sovereign LORD is my strength; he makes my feet like the feet of a deer, he enables me to go on the heights" (NIV). You, Lord, "shall subdue the people under us, and the nations under our feet" (Psalm 47:3). Also, Your words, Lord, declare that my child has been given "authority to trample on snakes and scorpions and to overcome all the power of the enemy; nothing [by any means] will harm [my child]" (Luke 10:19 NIV). I thank You that "the God of peace will soon crush Satan under [my child's] feet. The grace of our Lord Jesus" is with my child (Romans 16:20 NIV).

8

Blessed Rest

❧

As my child rested all through each and every night, I felt Your goodness toward him. It brought peace and security to my heart as I watched him sleeping. The peace that surpasses all understanding guards our hearts and minds through You, Lord Jesus (Philippians 4:7).

You take such pleasure in Your children. You are well-pleased with my child. You call us Your beloved. I thank You, Lord Jesus, that You give my beloved child sweet sleep. Your Word says in Proverbs 3:24, "When you lie down, you will not be afraid; yes, you will lie down and your sleep will be sweet." Your Word also says in Jeremiah 31:26 "Upon this I awaked, and beheld; and my sleep was sweet unto me."

As my child diligently seeks You, I ask, Lord Jesus, that You will reveal to him the secrets that only belong to those who diligently seek You (Hebrews 11:6). As my child sleeps, may You give him dreams and visions (Joel 2:28). As he sleeps, may You, holy Father, visit him through the night and show him the heavenly realm. Your Word says in Revelation 21:21: "The twelve gates were twelve pearls, each gate made of a single pearl. The great street of the city was of pure gold, like transparent glass" (NIV). I ask You, Lord Jesus, that you show my child the streets of gold, that he may walk in the realm of the spirit through the night as his body sleeps. Holy Father, I know that as my child sleeps, his spirit is not sleeping but is in heavenly places with You, beholding Your glory, walking the streets of gold.

Thank You for the sweet rest You give him. I can't help but notice that he looks even more beautiful when he is sleeping. May the hours of his rest be blessed.

9

Tears Transformed

❦❦

I thank You, Lord Jesus, that as my dear sweet child sheds tears and they roll down his cheeks, You place all of his tears in Your bottle, as Your Word says in Psalm 56:8: "You keep track of all my sorrows. You have collected all my tears in your bottle. You have recorded each one in your book" (NLT). It brings an assurance to know that not one tear goes unnoticed by You, Lord Jesus. You are a great Daddy who comforts every pain and knows every tear. You take my child in Your bosom, and he hears Your sweet whispers to him saying, "I love you." Psalm 103:11 says, "For as high as the heavens are above the earth, so great is his love for those who fear him" (NIV). Nothing can "separate us from the love of God, which is in Christ Jesus our Lord" (Romans 8:38-39). Second Chronicles 16:9 says, "For the eyes of the LORD run to and fro throughout the whole earth, to shew himself strong in the behalf of them whose heart is perfect toward him."

At times when my child is not able to express in words what he is feeling or what he is wanting, he expresses himself by crying. You, Lord Jesus, know how to help me understand my child better and acknowledge the things that bring him joy. I thank You, Lord Jesus, for the sweet Holy Spirit, which helps us in our weakness. "For we do not know what we should pray for as we ought, but the Spirit Himself makes intercession for us with groanings which cannot be uttered. Now He who searches the hearts knows what the mind of the Spirit is, because He makes intercession for the saints according to the will of God" (Romans 8:26-27 NKJV). I thank You, Lord Jesus, that through Your help, I am able to understand my child better.

I ask, Lord Jesus, that You help me fulfill my calling as a mother. Each day is recorded in Your book. Thank You, Lord Jesus, that You record everything in Your book, as it says in Revelation 20:12: "And I saw the dead, great and small, standing before the throne, and books were opened. Another book was opened, which is the book of life. The dead were judged according to what they had done as recorded in the books" (NIV). Thank You, Lord Jesus, for this sweet, precious child You entrusted to me. May I not cause any pain to him that will scar his soul, or wound his spirit, bringing tears to his eyes as a result of my actions. May I do my best in teaching him Your ways, so when the day comes that I stand before You and the books are opened, You will say to me, "Well done; you were a good mother." I will feel complete that I did my best to perform the task You gave me, to be a mother.

10

"The LORD Is My Strength"

T hank You, holy Father, for the strength You
have given to my child. He is mighty and strong,
active and full of zeal. He is more than a conqueror
(Romans 8:37), victorious in every way. We declare,
Lord Jesus, that "The LORD is my rock, my fortress
and my deliverer; my God is my rock, in whom I take
refuge. He is my shield and the horn of my salvation,
my stronghold" (Psalm 18:2 NIV).

You, Lord God, will arm my child with strength
and make his way perfect (Psalm 18:32). In a song, we
praise You and exalt You; we make a joyful melody,
for we are grateful for the strength You give. "Be
exalted, O LORD, in your strength; we will sing and
praise your might" (Psalm 21:13 NIV). Each day in
the journey my child takes is triumphant. It is a new
day filled with strength to abound. Psalm 28:7 says,
"The LORD is my strength and my shield; my heart

trusts in him, and I am helped. My heart leaps for joy and I will give thanks to him in song" (NIV). You, Lord Jesus, will give my child strength in the time of trouble (Psalm 37:39). I declare over my child the promise in Your Word in Psalm 138:7, which tells us, "Though I walk in the midst of trouble, you preserve my life; you stretch out your hand against the anger of my foes, with your right hand you save me" (NIV). I am assured that your outstretched arms are with my child in times of great difficulty (Exodus 6:6). Your arms, holy Father, are not too short to save my child, nor are your ears too dull to hear (Isaiah 59:1).

As my child grows and learns to go on each day, as he faces life's challenges and difficulties, I trust that my child rests in Your promises and learns to wait on You to renew his strength day by day. Your Word says in Isaiah 40:31: "But they that wait upon the LORD shall renew their strength; they shall mount up with wings as eagles; they shall run, and not be weary; and they shall walk, and not faint." My child is very well taken care of in Your arms, the arms of his loving Father.

11

Fulfillment of Destiny

Thank You, Holy Father, for this precious child You created for a special purpose, a special destiny. I declare that my child's destiny come forth. My dear child was created for a special purpose, to come to earth with a victorious assignment. The Word of the Lord says in Jeremiah 1:5, "Before I formed you in the womb I knew you, before you were born I set you apart; I appointed you as a prophet to the nations" (NIV). Thank You, Lord Jesus, that my child will fulfill and accomplish his calling You have assigned to him. As Your Word says: "My son, pay attention to what I say; listen closely to my words. Do not let them out of your sight, keep them within your heart; for they are life to those who find them and health to a man's whole body" (Proverbs 4:20-22 NIV). I bless my child, and I know that my child will be the one who carries out Your plan. Isaiah 46:11

says: "From the east I summon a bird of prey; from a far-off land, a man to fulfill my purpose. What I have said, that will I bring about; what I have planned, that will I do" (NIV).

I thank You, Lord Jesus, for the fulfillment of all Your promises in my child's life. I declare over my child the promise You made, Lord Jesus, in Isaiah 54:17, "No weapon that is formed against thee shall prosper; and every tongue that shall rise against thee in judgment thou shalt condemn."

I pronounce over my child that he is covered by Your blood. My child is sealed for You, Lord Jesus. He belongs to you (Ephesians 1:13). I proclaim the promises of the Lord over my beloved child, as it says in Jeremiah 29:11-13: "'For I know the plans I have for you,' declares the LORD, 'plans to prosper you and not to harm you, plans to give you hope and a future. Then you will call upon me and come and pray to me, and I will listen to you. You will seek me and find me when you seek me with all your heart'" (NIV).

My child has been preordained by the Lord Jesus Christ to be victorious. Life at times can be difficult. Challenges come and take us to a different course. I declare over my child the promise made by the Lord in Isaiah 14:27: "For the LORD Almighty has purposed, and who can thwart him? His hand is stretched out, and who can turn it back?" The Lord makes this promise regardless of all the disappointments that life brings, every mistake made, obstacles and setbacks, and all the evil forces of darkness. Nothing will stop or annul my child's destiny. I strike down the plans of the enemy who is trying to abort his destiny. I call my child's destiny to come forth and be fulfilled. I contend for the fulfillment of the destiny and purpose for creating my child to come to earth.

12

Healing Power

L ord Jesus, I thank You that my child is in
good health, as Your Word says in 3 John 1:2:
"Beloved, I wish above all things that thou mayest
prosper and be in health, even as thy soul prospereth."
I declare that my child is in good health. Lord, when
You died on the cross, You bore all of our sickness
and disease. First Peter 2:24 says, "Who his own self
bare our sins in his own body on the tree, that we,
being dead to sins, should live unto righteousness:
by whose stripes ye were healed." I am mindful
that supernatural healing can only come from You.
I declare what the Word of the Lord says in Psalm
103:2-3: "Bless the LORD, O my soul, and forget not
all His benefits: who forgives all your iniquities, who
heals all your diseases" (NKJV). Your Word says
ALL my diseases. ALL means ALL of my diseases.

Holy Father, You created my child, and You know how things should operate and what needs to be done to restore my child's health and ensure that my child's body, soul, and spirit operate at the highest level of efficiency. I thank You, Lord Jesus, that You came to earth. Through Your death, burial, and resurrection, You defeated sickness and death, giving us the opportunity to walk in divine health daily. Isaiah 53:5 tells us, "He was wounded for our transgressions, he was bruised for our iniquities: the chastisement of our peace was upon Him; and with his stripes we are healed." Thank You, Lord Jesus, for Your healing power. You are the Jehovah-Rophe, our Healer. Thank You, Lord Jesus, that my child will live a long and healthy life. Jeremiah 33:6 says, "I will heal them and reveal to them the abundance of peace and truth" (NKJV). I declare all Your promises on healing over my child, for Your Word is true, and I trust and stand on Your Word of promise. Jeremiah 17:14 says, "Heal me, O LORD, and I shall be healed" (NKJV). Jeremiah 30:17 says, "I will restore health to you and heal you of your wounds" (NKJV).

Thank You, Lord Jesus, that You have heard my prayer and seen my tears. Surely, You will heal my child. Second Kings 20:5 says "I have heard your prayer, I have seen your tears; surely I will heal you" (NKJV). Psalm 107:19-20 says: "They cried out to the LORD in their trouble, and He saved them out of their distresses. He sent His word and healed them, and delivered them from their destructions" (NKJV).

I thank You, Lord Jesus, that my child walks in divine health. I speak Your Word over my child, as it says in Isaiah 58:8: "Your light shall break forth like the morning, your healing shall spring forth speedily, and your righteousness shall go before you; the glory of the LORD shall be your rear guard" (NKJV). I bless my child's body, for it is the temple of God and Your Spirit lives in my child (1 Corinthians 3:16-17). Lord Jesus, in view of Your mercy, my child offers his body as a living sacrifice, holy and pleasing to you. This is my child's spiritual act of worship (Romans 12:1).

Thank You, holy Father, for every part of my child's body You created. In the book of Isaiah, You tell us, Lord Jesus, that You will not forget my child, even if I, his mother, forget him. You have carved him in your hands. "Can a mother forget the baby at her breast and have no compassion on the child she has borne? Though she may forget, I will not forget you! See, I have engraved you on the palms of my hands; your walls are ever before me" (Isaiah 49:15-16 NIV).

13

Healthy Friendships

Holy Father, I pray that You will give my child divine connection with the right type of friends. I thank You, Lord Jesus, that You will draw my child to be around the highest quality of people and the ones whose hearts are aimed toward You, as Your Word says in Proverbs 27:17, "As iron sharpens iron, so a man sharpens the countenance of his friend" (NKJV). They will be a good influence. They will bring laughter and joy to one another. "Ointment and perfume delight the heart, and the sweetness of a man's friend gives delight by hearty counsel" (Proverbs 27:9 NKJV). We sing songs of gladness to You, for the joy of the Lord is our strength (Psalm 28:7; Nehemiah 8:10).

Lord Jesus, the gift a friend brings is one of the most treasured memories cherished by a child growing up. You made us, Lord, to need each other.

As You made the body, needing each part, so each of us needs one another to help us grow and mature, as stated in 1 Corinthians 12:19-27 (NLT):

How strange a body would be if it had only one part! Yes, there are many parts, but only one body. The eye can never say to the hand, "I don't need you." The head can't say to the feet, "I don't need you." In fact, some parts of the body that seem weakest and least important are actually the most necessary. And the parts we regard as less honorable are those we clothe with the greatest care. So we carefully protect those parts that should not be seen, while the more honorable parts do not require this special care. So God has put the body together such that extra honor and care are given to those parts that have less dignity. This makes for harmony among the members, so that all the members care for each other. If one part suffers, all the parts suffer with it, and if one part is honored, all the parts are glad. All of you together are Christ's body, and each of you is a part of it.

Father, I ask You to give my child discernment to separate himself from anyone who will not be a good influence (1 Corinthians 5:13). Enable him to be a forgiving person and not carry grudges or hold things in his heart against others. Lord, You've said in Your Word that "he who hates his brother is in darkness and walks in darkness, and does not know where he is going, because the darkness has blinded his eyes" (1 John 2:11 NKJV). I pray that my child will never be blinded by the darkness of unforgiveness, but continually walk in the light of forgiveness. Lord, help my child to be obedient to Your words in Matthew 7:1-5:

> Do not judge, or you too will be judged. For in the same way you judge others, you will be judged, and with the measure you use, it will be measured to you. Why do you look at the speck of sawdust in your brother's eye and pay no attention to the plank in your own eye? How can you say to your brother, "Let me take the speck out of your eye," when all the time there is a plank in your own eye? You hypocrite, first take the plank out of your own eye, and then you will see clearly to remove the speck from your brother's eye.

May my child not judge or show contempt for anyone, but remember that "we shall all stand before the judgment seat of Christ" (Romans 14:10). Enable him to love his enemies, bless those who curse him, do good to those who hate him, and pray for those who spitefully use him and persecute him (Matthew 5:44).

Finally, Lord Jesus, I ask that my relationship with my child will be a good, long-lasting relationship centered on You. Thank You, Lord Jesus, that my child loves me unconditionally, regardless of the mistakes I have made in raising him and the wrong examples he has seen me show. Through the challenges and obstacles we have experienced, my child has always hugged me and told me he loves me. My heart melts with the love I receive from my children. Seal and protect our relationship, holy Father. I bless my child, and I pray that in his heart, he will honor his father and mother so that he will live long and be blessed in his life (Exodus 20:12).

14

His Protective Arms
🌿

Lord Jesus, as a mother, one of my greatest fears is my child getting hurt. Holy Father, my child is in Your care. You are a good Father. You are the best Daddy; You protect and care for Your children. My child is in Your protective arms. My trust is in You, Lord. My assurance is in Your promise. "The LORD is my rock and my fortress and my deliverer; My God, my strength, in whom I will trust; My shield and the horn of my salvation, my stronghold. I will call upon the LORD, who is worthy to be praised; So shall I be saved from my enemies" (Psalm 18:2-3 NKJV). Isaiah 54:17 tells us, "'No weapon formed against you shall prosper, and every tongue which rises against you in judgment You shall condemn. This is the heritage of the servants of the LORD, and their righteousness is from Me,' says the LORD" (NKJV). Thank You, holy Father, that my child is covered by Your blood. The blood of the Lord Jesus Christ protects my child. Mark 16:18 tells us, "They shall take up serpents; and if they drink any deadly thing, it shall not hurt them."

There is nothing more powerful than Your words of protection. I thank You, Lord Jesus, that nothing by any means can harm my child. You cover and seal my child; under Your wings, my child finds refuge. You have my child in the palm of Your hand (Isaiah 49:6). I am not always near to protect my child, but You keep a close watch over my child. You are the best shepherd; You protect and guide Your sheep. You are the Good Shepherd. You lay Your life down for the sheep (John 10:11). You know Your sheep, and Your sheep know Your voice (John 10:14). Only You, holy Father, can protect my child, for Your hands are stretched out toward my child (Isaiah 45:12).

Your goodness and mercy follow my child wherever he goes (Psalm 23:6). Even if my child walks through the dark valley, You are there, Lord (Psalm 23:4). You have my child engraved on Your palms (Isaiah 49:16). You command Your angels to take guard and protect my child in all his ways (Psalm 91:11). You have promised that You will never leave us or forsake us (Hebrews 13:5). I ask, Lord Jesus, that You protect my child from the evil one. I speak Your words, Lord Jesus, over my child, as Your Word says in John 10:28-29: "And I give them eternal life, and they shall never perish; neither shall anyone snatch them out of My hand. My Father, who has given *them* to Me, is greater than all; and no one is able to snatch *them* out of My Father's hand" (NKJV).

Only You alone, Father, can take my child to places that he can only dream of, for You are always guiding him and protecting him to receive the best of life You want him to have. You are always with my child, "even to the end of the age" (Matthew 28:20). You, holy Father, are my child's strength, and You are his saving refuge (Psalm 28:8).

As I hold my child in my arms and rock him in my rocking chair, I pray over him Psalm 91 (NKJV). I consider this Psalm my life insurance psalm from the Word of the Lord Jesus Christ:

¹ He who dwells in the secret place of the Most High
   Shall abide under the shadow of the Almighty.
² I will say of the LORD, "He is my refuge and my fortress;
   My God, in Him I will trust."
³ Surely He shall deliver you from the snare of the fowler
   And from the perilous pestilence.
⁴ He shall cover you with His feathers,
   And under His wings you shall take refuge;
   His truth shall be your shield and buckler.
⁵ You shall not be afraid of the terror by night,
   Nor of the arrow that flies by day,
⁶ Nor of the pestilence that walks in darkness,
   Nor of the destruction that lays waste at noonday.

7 A thousand may fall at your side,
    And ten thousand at your right hand;
    But it shall not come near you.
8 Only with your eyes shall you look,
    And see the reward of the wicked.
9 Because you have made the LORD, who is my
    refuge,
    Even the Most High, your dwelling place,
10 No evil shall befall you,
    Nor shall any plague come near your
    dwelling;
11 For He shall give His angels charge over you,
    To keep you in all your ways.
12 In their hands they shall bear you up,
    Lest you dash your foot against a stone.
13 You shall tread upon the lion and the cobra,
    The young lion and the serpent you shall
    trample underfoot.
14 "Because he has set his love upon Me, there-
    fore I will deliver him;
    I will set him on high, because he has known
    My name.
15 He shall call upon Me, and I will answer him;
    I will be with him in trouble;
    I will deliver him and honor him.
16 With long life I will satisfy him,
    And show him My salvation."

15

Cast Out Fear

ord Jesus, You are a God of light and love.
In You there is no fear, no darkness, and love
dwells. Perfect love that comes from You casts out
fear (1 John 4:18). You are the light of the world,
Lord Jesus; in You there is no darkness (1 John 1:5).
Darkness does not come from you; it comes from
the evil one, whose plan is to steal, kill, and destroy
(John 10:10). Lord Jesus, You have given us authority
over the spirit of darkness. Your spirit dwells in us.
Whatever we bind on earth is bound, and whatever
we loose on earth is loosed (Matthew 18:18).

Lord Jesus, I ask You to help my child overcome thoughts that say, "I can't do it," "I am afraid,"
"There's a strange creature," and "I am scared." Lord,
help my child to remember the words you spoke in
Isaiah 54:14: "In righteousness shalt thou be established: thou shalt be far from oppression; for thou

shalt not fear: and from terror; for it shall not come near thee."

Protect my child from the spirit of condemnation. When he cries and feels bad that he sinned, let him know of Your forgiveness and that there is no condemnation in You. We are the righteousness in Christ (Romans 8:1). Help me, Lord Jesus, to teach my child to call on You when he is afraid, as Your Word says in Psalm 34:4: "I sought the LORD, and he heard me, and delivered me from all my fears." Let my child be strong and courageous, just as You, Lord, told Joshua: "Have I not commanded you? Be strong and of good courage; do not be afraid, nor be dismayed, for the LORD your God is with you wherever you go" (Joshua 1:9 NKJV). I thank You, Lord Jesus, that You are my child's rear guard, as Isaiah 52:12 states: "But you will not leave in haste or go in flight; for the LORD will go before you, the God of Israel will be your rear guard."

Fear enters through what he thinks and what he sees. Lord Jesus, help my child to replace the images of fear with images of faith pictures, as You say in Romans 12:21: "Be not overcome of evil, but overcome evil with good." Let him see the beauty of Your creation and not the dark and gloomy reports that others may bring, just as Joshua and Caleb brought back a good report about the land in Canaan, saying that it is a land flowing with milk and honey and surely the Lord will help us overcome the giants in the land (Numbers 14:8-9). Let my child see things in the sight of the Lord. Holy Father, You have told us, "Fear not, little flock; for it is your Father's good pleasure to give you the kingdom" (Luke 12:32). You are a good God who loves to give good gifts to Your children. You know our needs, and You provide (Matthew 7:11).

Lord Jesus, help my child to use the gifts and talents that You gave him wisely—and not let fear come in and control him and hide his talents and hinder him from using his God-given abilities for Your kingdom glory. In Matthew 25:14, we have the parable of the talents. The servant who received one talent hid it because he was afraid. He missed out on his ministry in this life, and the position and reward the Lord intended him to have in the next dispensation, because of fear. That fear was based on a lie of the enemy. There is no reason to believe that our Lord is a "hard man." The servant's own mouth condemned him when he said, "And I was afraid, and went and hid thy talent" (v. 25).

Lord Jesus, help my child to focus on You and to look unto You, "the author and finisher of our faith" (Hebrews 12:2). You, Lord Jesus, are near to those who call upon You (Psalm 145:18). As my child cries to You, Lord Jesus, You will rescue him. You, Lord Jesus, will hold my child's right hand, "saying unto thee, Fear not; I will help thee" (Isaiah 41:13). As my child feels Your hand, Lord, it will comfort him, and he will see there is no need to fear and how easy it is to walk in faith. May Your Word, Lord Jesus, penetrate every fiber of my child's being, convincing him that Your love for him is far greater than anything he faces, and nothing can separate him from it.

Thank You, Lord Jesus, that my child will recognize and practice Your divine presence next to him at all times. He will fix his imagination on You, Lord, eternal and shining in Your splendor. "Thou wilt keep him in perfect peace, whose mind is stayed on thee: because he trusteth in thee" (Isaiah 26:3).

16

Grant Favor

L ord Jesus, You have blessed me beyond what I
can ask or imagine. You have blessed me with
two beautiful angel-like children. I could not ask You
for anything more. It is truly a blessing to be granted
life and favor. Life and favor are both gifts from You,
Lord Jesus: "Thou hast granted me life and favour,
and thy visitation hath preserved my spirit" (Job
10:12).

You are gracious. You are the Lord God, merciful
and gracious (Exodus 34:6). I pray, Lord Jesus, that
my child increases in favor with You and with man.
I ask, Lord Jesus, for great grace over my child (Acts
4:33). Make the greater realms of favor available for
my child to walk in. Allow my child to be able to
enter into the realm of abundance of favor, as stated
in Romans 5:17: "much more they which receive
abundance of grace and of the gift of righteous-

ness shall reign in life by one, Jesus Christ." Father, You are the God of abundance. You are "able to do exceeding abundantly above all that we ask or think" (Ephesians 3:20). I ask, Lord Jesus, for favor to be multiplied and for my child to receive an abundance of grace multiplied. "Grace and peace be multiplied unto you through the knowledge of God, and of Jesus our Lord" (2 Peter 1:2). Lord, your favor is limitless. I ask, Lord Jesus, that this generation that my child walks in will have levels of favor that others have never walked in and others have never experienced before, as Proverbs 3:3-4 says: "Let not mercy and truth forsake thee: bind them about thy neck; write them upon the table of thine heart: So shalt thou find favour and good understanding in the sight of God and man."

I ask, Lord Jesus, that my child sow seeds of kindness and mercy toward others, so that my child will reap kindness and mercy from others as well. Help my child understand that as you sow goodness, you will reap a harvest of goodness (Psalm 112:4-5, 9). May he be trustworthy, a reliable person that You, Lord, can count on to faithfully obey Your Word. May You find no corruption in my child. May he be trustworthy and neither corrupt, nor negligent (Daniel 6:4). May You call my child Your greatly beloved (Daniel 10:11). I ask, Lord Jesus, that You help my child to live a life that is honest before God and man (2 Corinthians 8:21). Father, You love honestly. Honesty is truthfulness and sincerity. Favor is release to those who are sincere in their walk with

God. "Grace [favor] be with all them that love our Lord Jesus Christ in sincerity" (Ephesians 6:24).

Lord Jesus, help my child to increase in the knowledge of You. "Grace [favor] and peace be multiplied unto you through the knowledge of God, and of Jesus our Lord" (2 Peter 1:2). May I be a good example for my child to encourage him to study the Word of God. May he read good books, learn more about the things of God, increase in wisdom, associate with wise people. "For whoso findeth me findeth life, and shall obtain favour of the LORD" (Proverbs 8:35). I ask, Lord Jesus, that Your Spirit rest upon my child, as Isaiah 11:2 states: "The Spirit of the LORD shall rest upon him, the spirit of wisdom and understanding, the spirit of counsel and might, the spirit of knowledge and of the fear of the LORD." Lord Jesus, I know that this is Your desire for my child. "For thou art the glory of their strength: and in thy favour our horn shall be exalted" (Psalm 89:17). I ask for favor for my child, for Your Word says we have not because we ask not. Father, You delight in giving favor to Your children. In humility, I ask, Lord, for You to give Your grace to the humble (James 4:6). I thank You, Lord Jesus, that my child will enjoy a "favored child" status from You, his heavenly Father. My child will know and be confident that he is Your favorite child, and Your favor will overflow in his life. I praise You, Lord Jesus, and give You glory.

My Personal Prayer to the Lord

Lord Jesus, You are the Lover of my soul. You are the Prince of Peace, the everlasting Father. Every good and perfect gift, each of my children, has come from You. I am forever grateful for the gift of life You have given me. You have given me the honor and the privilege to be the mother of two beautiful angel-like children. I could not ask for anything more. You have rewarded me far more than I could ask or imagine. You have given me more than any woman on this earth has received.

As a mother to these two children, I promise to take care of them. I will do my best to bring them up in Your ways, Your commands, and Your statutes. I will do my best to be a good example to them, to live by Galatians 5:22-23, which says: "The fruit of the Spirit is love, joy, peace, patience, kindness, goodness, faithfulness, gentleness and self-control" (NIV). With the help of the sweet Holy Spirit, I know that I will be a good mother, faithful, and I will offer myself as a sacrifice for the best interest of my children. Holy Father, help me fulfill my destiny that You have given me to raise John Sundar and Grace Jayashree. In Your name, Lord Jesus, I pray. Amen.

Father, I dedicate this Scripture to You:

Song of Solomon 5:10-16 (NIV)

[10] My lover is radiant and ruddy,
   outstanding among ten thousand.

[11] His head is purest gold;
   his hair is wavy
   and black as a raven.

[12] His eyes are like doves
   by the water streams,
   washed in milk,
   mounted like jewels.

[13] His cheeks are like beds of spice
   yielding perfume.
   His lips are like lilies
   dripping with myrrh.

[14] His arms are rods of gold
   set with chrysolite.
   His body is like polished ivory
   decorated with sapphires.

[15] His legs are pillars of marble
   set on bases of pure gold.
   His appearance is like Lebanon,
   choice as its cedars.

[16] His mouth is sweetness itself;
   he is altogether lovely.
   This is my lover, this my friend,
   O daughters of Jerusalem.

A Mother's Diary

🐾

Each child wants to know all about himself or herself. Each child loves to hear stories about what he or she was like growing up. This workbook will help you keep a log of stories to tell your child when he or she sits in your lap and says to you, "Mama, tell me about me. Mama, tell me, when I was little, how did I act? What were the things I did, Mama? Tell me, Mama, what were my favorite things?"

It is a true blessing to recall and share with a child all the sweet memories only a mother can tell. A mother knows her child in a very special way. A child's mother can perhaps best recall the child's uniqueness and creativity. No one can tell the story like Mama can.

For My Child

To my dear child, _____, I love you very dearly. I would like to tell you the story of what it was like when you were born, the changes in your physical body as you grew, and the memorable things you did. I treasured every moment I spent with you. I recorded things you did. I want to give this diary as a gift to you for you to remember that you are very special to me.

The day you were born:
_____ (month) _____ (date)
_____ (year)

1. This is how I felt before the delivery:

2. This is how I felt during the delivery:

3. This is how I felt after the delivery:

4. I gave birth to you at _____. This is what happened:

5. On the first night of your birth, we slept together. This is what happened:

6. The first day you were born, I fed you my breast milk. This is what happened:

7. The first time I held you in my arms, this is how I felt:

8. The first night you slept at the hospital, I could not get my eyes off you. I watched you very closely. This is how I felt: _____. And this is what happened:

9. The first day we left the hospital and you were taken out into the world, it was the first time you rode in the car to go home. This is who was with us and what happened:

10. This was the first day you were home from the hospital: _____. And this is what happened:

11. The first night you slept in your own bed at home, this is what happened:

12. These were the thoughts in my mind as you were sleeping:

13. As the months went by, there were nights when you would not go to sleep. This is how I felt, and this is what happened:

14. You loved being rocked in the rocking chair, and you loved falling asleep in my arms as I swayed you. This is what it was like:

15. This was the song I sang to you: _____.

16. This is what your hair was like when you were born:

17. As the days went by, your hair changed in this way:

18. The first time you got your hair cut, this is where we went and how excited I felt:

19. The first time I glanced at your eyes, this is what it was like:

20. After a few months, this is what your eyes were like:

21. This is what your nose was like when you were born:

22. After a few months, this is what your nose was like:

23. This is what your ears were like when you were born:

24. After a few months, this is what your ears were like:

25. This is what your lips were like when you were born:

26. The first time I kissed your lips, this is how I felt:

27. Your first word was_____. This is what it was like as you said your first word:

28. The first song you sang was _____.
This is what it was like as you sang your first song:

29. Your favorite song was _____.

30. The first time I held your hands, this is how I felt:

31. Your hands were closed like a fist. I tried to open them, and this is what I thought to myself:

32. As the months went by, this is what your hands were like:

33. The first time you pulled on my hair, my earrings, and my clothes, this is what it was like:

34. The first time you clapped your hands was when we were:

35. The first time I kissed your feet, this is how I felt:

36. This is what your feet looked like:

37. As the months went by, your feet grew stronger and bigger. I placed the first pair of shoes on your feet. This is what happened and the shoes you had:

38. The first time you started to crawl, this is where you were: _____. And this is what it was like:

39. You started crawling when you were _____ months old. I had to keep a close watch on you. This is what happened:

40. When you took your first step, this is where you were: _____. And this is what it was like:

41. You fell a few times and got up again to try to walk. This is what happened:

42. You held my hands as you learned to walk. This is how I felt:

43. As the months went by, you started to run, and I had to chase after you. This is what it was like:

44. The tears you shed are very precious to me. The first time I remember you crying, I did not know what to do. I was very protective of you. It would break my heart each time I saw tears roll down your cheeks. The first time you cried, this is what it was like:

45. This is how I felt and what I did:

46. As you grew in strength and stature, I made declarations that you will be mighty and strong, great in stature, and a warrior in the kingdom of God. As time went by, you started to play with your siblings and friends. This was your favorite toy and your favorite game:

47. I prayed every day for your destiny to come forth, to be revealed to you, and to unfold in due time. I noticed things you did, how you reacted, and the things you enjoyed. This is what it was like, and I discovered your personality was:

48. People noticed you and how special you were and are. These were all the nice things they said about you:

49. These were the prophesies spoken over you:

50. These were the men of God who laid their blessing hands over you to bless you as you grew up and to discover your destiny, your calling and gifts: